A Nation of Inventors

Researching American History

edited by

JoAnne Weisman Deitch

Advertised in 1899, the "electropathic belt" was thought to cure a variety of ailments. (Library of Congress)

Discovery Enterprises, Ltd.
Carlisle, Massachusetts

All rights reserved. No part of this book may be reproduced, stored in a retrieval system, or transmitted in any form or by any means, electronic, mechanical, photocopied, recorded, or otherwise, without prior written permission of the authors or publisher, except for brief quotes and illustrations used for review purposes.

First Edition © Discovery Enterprises, Ltd., Carlisle, MA 2001

ISBN 1-57960-077-8

Library of Congress Catalog Card Number 00-110344

10 9 8 7 6 5 4 3 2 1

Printed in the United States of America

Subject Reference Guide:

Title: *American Inventors*
Series: *Researching American History*
edited by JoAnne Weisman Deitch

Nonfiction
Primary source documents re:
Inventors - American History

Credits:

Illustrations are credited where
they appear in the book.

Acknowledgments:

Special thanks to David C. King
for his research, editing and introductions
excerpted from
The Age of Technology: 19th Century American Inventors,
Copyright, Discovery Enterprises, Ltd., Carlisle, MA 1997
The Roaring Twenties,
Copyright, Discovery Enterprises, Ltd., Carlisle, MA 1997
and *Thomas Alva Edison: The King of Inventors*
Copyright, Discovery Enterprises, Ltd., Lowell, MA 1995
Several of the introductory passages and primary source documents
in this book rely heavily upon and excerpt his work.

Contents

About the Series 4
   Reading the Historical Documents 4

Introduction by JoAnne Weisman Deitch 5
   "The Whispering Telephone" 5
   "The World can not keep pace..." 6

Inventors of the 18th Century 7
   Benjamin Franklin 7
   Patents 10
   Thomas Jefferson 11
   Eli Whitney 12
   Benjamin Banneker 14

Farming Inventions of the 19th Century 16
   John Deere 16
   The McCormick Reaper 16
   Joseph Glidden 18
   George Washington Carver 19

Industrial Inventions of the 19th Century 20
   Samuel Colt's Assembly Line 20
   Morse and the Telegraph 22
   Elisha Otis: Conquering Vertical Space 24
   The Inventive Spirit Takes Hold 25
   Bell's Telephone 26
   Thomas Alva Edison 30
   Lewis Howard Latimer 34

Life-Altering Inventions of the 20th Century 35
   Henry Ford 35
   The Wright Brothers 38

The Computer Age 42
   Herman Hollerith: The Electric Sorting and Tabulating Machine 42
   Grace Hopper 44
   Robotics 46
   And, they still keep coming up with new ideas... 48

Research Activities/Things to do 50

Suggested Further Reading 56

Suggested Web Sites 56

About the Series

Researching American History is a series of books which introduces various topics and periods in our nation's history through the study of primary source documents.

Reading the Historical Documents

On the following pages you'll find words written by people during or soon after the time of the events. This is firsthand information about what life was like back then. Illustrations are also created to record history. These historical documents are called **primary source materials**.

At first, some things written in earlier times may seem difficult to understand. Language changes over the years, and the objects and activities described might be unfamiliar. Also, spellings were sometimes different. Below is a model which describes how we help with these challenges.

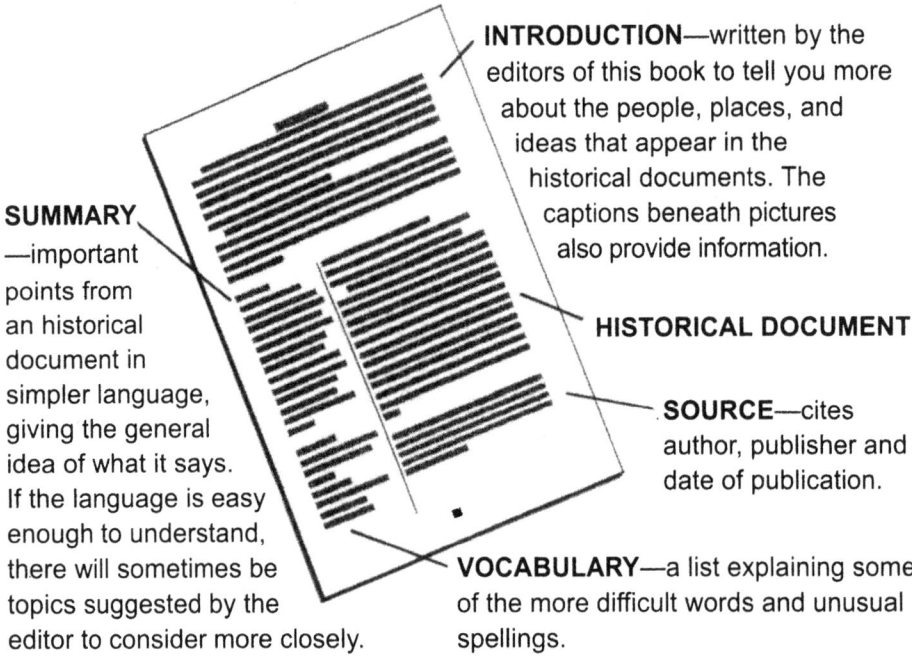

INTRODUCTION—written by the editors of this book to tell you more about the people, places, and ideas that appear in the historical documents. The captions beneath pictures also provide information.

HISTORICAL DOCUMENT

SOURCE—cites author, publisher and date of publication.

VOCABULARY—a list explaining some of the more difficult words and unusual spellings.

SUMMARY—important points from an historical document in simpler language, giving the general idea of what it says. If the language is easy enough to understand, there will sometimes be topics suggested by the editor to consider more closely.

In these historical documents, you may see three periods (…) called an ellipsis. It means that the editor has left out some words or sentences. You may see some words in brackets, such as [and]. These are words the editor has added to make the meaning clearer. When you use a document in a paper you're writing, you should include any ellipses and brackets it contains, just as you see them here. Be sure to give complete information about the author, title, and publisher of anything that was written by someone other than you.

Introduction

by JoAnne Weisman Deitch

Americans are a curious and entrepreneurial lot. Upon their arrival in the "New World," the Colonists had to find creative ways to make their lives easier and their work more productive in their new surroundings.

Inventions, then and now, usually begin with an idea on how to do or make something better, or how to find a solution to a particular problem. One of the most illustrious and accomplished inventors of the colonial period, Benjamin Franklin, was often told, jokingly, that he was lazy, because he was constantly trying to design devices that would make his life easier or more comfortable. He was extraordinarily successful at it, too!

Some creative people did not actually produce new inventions, but incorporated them in fiction. (Science fiction writers are still popular today, and some of their fantastic inventions actually come into being years after they've described them in books.) In 1890, Alvan D. Brock reported on the writing of Edward Bellamy, an author of romances in the late 1800s, who incorporated descriptions of inventions that were to come in the future.

"The Whispering Telephone"

...In another prophetic romance one of the characters is pictured as drawing a small instrument from his pocket, and attaching it to an electric wire, holding conversations with persons at a distance.

There be those who are now "looking forward," watching with eager eyes and listening with strained ears to the heralding of the accomplishments of the electrical marvels foretold in these romances. To the man or woman of quick imagination there is nothing impossible or even improbable in these narratives.

...There is today in this city, and has been for many weeks,—the writer first saw it on the first day of June, 1890,—the telephone of the future a perfection of all preceding telephones, that is destined to supplant them all. ...it is definitely superior in all points of mere mechanical con-

(continued on next page)

Summary:

In another story that predicts the future, one of the characters takes a small device from his pocket and connects it to a wire, and talks to someone far away.

Today, I saw a telephone of the future. It had the transmitter and the receiver in the same phone, and was so small you could just disconnect it and put it away.

Vocabulary:

heralding = announcing
romance = a long narrative story
supplant = replace

Consider this:
Have you ever had an idea for an invention?

Was it based on something that exists now, or was it a totally new concept?

Vocabulary:
infinitely = having no limits

struction ;...its cost is infinitely less than that of any other telephone; ...it is both transmitter and receiver in the same instrument...it is infinitely more convenient and adjustable to the needs of the user;...it can be detached from its connections in an instant, put in the pocket, carried to any point where there is a wire, and almost as quickly connected and operated, or it can be locked in a drawer until needed for use;....

Source: Alvan Brock, "The Whispering Telephone," *Overland Monthly and Out West Magazine*, vol. 16, iss. 92, San Francisco, 1890, pp. 122-6.

When you read, further on in this book, about Alexander Graham Bell's telephone—remarkable, yet cumbersome—you'll recognize the imaginative talents of the man that envisioned a portable phone like the one described above.

It seems as though as soon as one invention was "up and running," others were at work trying to improve upon it, or replace it with a better, faster, cheaper, easier device. During the 19th century, new ideas were implemented —fast and furiously. Magazines and journals of all kinds kept the public up-to-date on the latest technology. You would be correct in equating it with the widespread availability of technology magazines and television documentaries of today. Following is an article describing the rapid advances in technology from *Appletons' Journal* in 1881.

Consider this:
The 19th century introduced one new invention after another. Why do you think so many new ideas came along at this particular time in American history?

"The world can not keep pace..."

The world can not keep pace with the scientific surprises of this age. Before sufficient time has elapsed to make one startling invention familiar, another equally astonishing is already the subject of lectures and newspaper articles. Before the telephone, the microphone, and the phonograph have found their way into common use, a still more extraordinary instrument is announced, one of which the results are as unexpected by the scientific as they are incredible to the ordinary mind.

Source: "The Photophone," *Appletons' Journal*, vol. 10, iss. 56, New York, February, 1881. Found on http://www.hti.umich.edu/cgi/m/moajrnl/

Inventors of the 18th Century

Benjamin Franklin

Benjamin Franklin (1706-1790), statesman, printer, publisher, and inventor, was one of the first to successfully study the properties of electricity. Perhaps the most widely-known story about his inventions concerns his experiment with lightning. The young man with Franklin is his son.

Franklin's experiment, June 1752, from a Currier and Ives print.

Following is an excerpt from a radio story about Ben Franklin's lightning experiment, which led to his invention of the lightning rod. Franklin and his 21-year-old son crossed a meadow to a hillside outside of Philadelpia on that fateful night in the summer of 1752.

Things to do:
This passage was written for a radio show, as a dramatization of Franklin's lightning experiment. Take one of the documents in this book and rewrite it for a radio show of your own creation.

…As the rain began, the two men got the kite up into the air. In order to withstand the storm, it had been made of silk with strong cedar crossbars…. Franklin attached the end of the line to a silk ribbon, to which he had tied a key. "The sparks should stream off the end of the key," he explained to his son. "And if we get sparks, that proves that lightning *is* electricity."

…They had to wait until the line was drenched and then—

"Look!" cried Franklin. The strands of hemp were bristling and sparks were beginning to crackle off the key. Their experiment was a success! Electricity was flowing down the line and off the key!

Once Franklin discovered the electrical fluid in lightning, he lost no time putting his discovery to practical use…innumerable homes, churches and public buildings had been burned when struck by lightning. Yet those fires would not have occurred if the buildings had been provided with lightning-rods to conduct the electricity into the ground.

…Before that, whenever a home had been struck by lightning, his volunteer fire department [another Franklin invention] had had to rush to the spot with their leather buckets, to save lives and property. Often they had arrived too late. But now, when a thunder-gust came in the middle of the night, he could remember that the lightning rod would take care of it, and comfortably go back to sleep.

Source: Carl Cramer, ed., *Cavalcade of America,* New York: Crown Publishers, 1956, p. 57. Based on the broadcasts of "The Cavalcade of America" radio series.

Franklin discovered and invented many things in his lifetime. *(See page 51)* One of his creations, still in use today, is the Franklin stove. The following excerpt comes from Franklin's *Autobiography*.

The Franklin Stove

...In order of time, I should have mentioned before, that having, in 1742, invented an open stove for the better warming of rooms, and at the same time saving fuel, as the fresh air admitted was warmed in entering, I made a present of the model to Mr. Robert Grace, one of my early friends, who, having an iron-furnace, found the casting of the plates for these stoves a profitable thing, as they were growing in demand.

To promote that demand, I wrote and published a pamphlet, entitled "An Account of the new-invented Pennsylvania Fireplaces; wherein their Construction and Manner of Operation is particularly explained; their Advantages above every other Method of warming Rooms demonstrated; and all Objections that have been raised against the Use of them answered and obviated," etc.

This pamphlet had a good effect. Gov'r. Thomas was so pleas'd with the construction of this stove, as described in it, that he offered to give me a patent for the sole vending of them for a term of years; but I declin'd it from a principle which has ever weighed with me on such occasions, viz., That, as we enjoy great advantages from the inventions of others, we should be glad of an opportunity to serve others by any invention of ours; and this we should do freely and generously.

Source: Benjamin Franklin, *Autobiography*, Chapter 10. Found on http://lcweb2.loc.gov/cgi-bin/query/

Consider this:
Most inventors are eager to obtain patents for their inventions. What do you think about Franklin's attitude about not getting a patent for his stove?

Vocabulary:
obviate = dispose of
viz. = that is; namely

Patents
Congress, Empowered by the Constitution

In Article I, Section 8, Clause 8, the Constitution empowers Congress "To promote the progress of science and useful arts by securing for limited times to authors and inventors the exclusive right to their respective writings and discoveries." Patent law must carefully balance the rights of the inventor to profit from his or her invention (through the grant of a temporary monopoly) against the needs of society at large to benefit from new ideas.

The patent bill of 1790 enabled the government to patent "any useful art, manufacture, engine, machine, or device, or any instrument thereon not before known or used." The patent act of 1793 gave the secretary of state the power to issue a patent to anyone who presented working drawings, a written description, a model, and paid an application fee. Over time, the requirements and procedures have changed. Today the U. S. Patent and Trademark Office is under the auspices of the Commerce Department.

Source: www.nara.gov/education/

Disclosure of the Invention

The patent system encourages disclosure and discourages secrecy, thus ensuring a free flow of information essential in a democracy and free enterprise system. …a patent creates a legal monopoly for a number of years. When the term of the patent (now 20 years) is expired, the invention becomes part of the public domain…. Drawings and specifications of the patent become part of the public record. Today the Records of the Patent and Trademark Office are in Record Group 241 at the National Archives at College Park, MD.

Source: This article was written by Joan Brodsky Schur, a teacher at Village Community School in New York, NY, and can be found on http://www.nara.gov/education/

Mary Kies: First American Female Patent Holder

Women in the 19th century had little opportunity to be inventive. Working in the home gave them almost no chance to gain skills in mechanics or in the use of power sources like electricity and steam.

The Patent Act of 1790 opened the door for any person, male or female, to patent an invention. However, in many states, women could not own property independent of their husbands, so they didn't bother to patent their inventions. Mary Kies broke that pattern as the first woman to receive a U. S. patent on May 15th, 1809 for a method of weaving straw with silk.

Source: Found on http://www.inventorsmuseum.com

Thomas Jefferson

When the Patent Office celebrated its one hundredth birthday, a bust of Thomas Jefferson [1743-1826] was dedicated, recognizing him as one of the fathers of that institution. Probably no more eminent or more reluctant person held the post as examiner of American patents. As Secretary of State, Jefferson also inherited the Patent Office, a governmental function which he was originally opposed to philosophically. But, he probably did more to encourage the flourishing of American invention through his direction of the Patent Office than any other American in history. The patent system he created remains the basis for the patent system of today. Much of the present structure, rules, and guidelines, were established by him.

Jefferson...acquired a taste for continental cooking while serving as American minister to France in the 1780s. When he returned to the United States in 1790, he brought with him a French cook and many recipes for French, Italian, and other *au courant* cookery. Jefferson not only served his guests the best European wines, but he liked to dazzle them with delights such as ice cream, peach flambé, macaroni, and macaroons. This drawing of a macaroni machine, with the sectional view showing holes from which dough could be extruded, reflects Jefferson's curious mind and his interest and aptitude in mechanical matters.

Source: Gerard W. Gawalt, Manuscript Division, Library of Congress. Found on http://earlyamerica.com/review/winter2000/jefferson.html

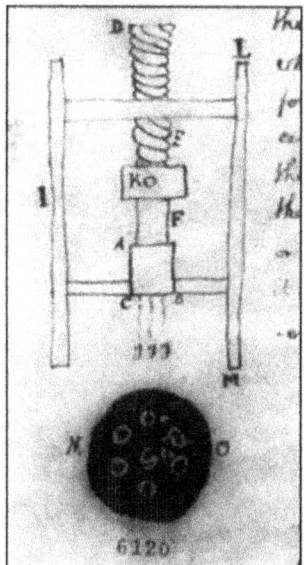

Jefferson's patent application drawing

Consider this:
Jefferson learned a lot in Europe, and brought ideas home with him. He was able to recreate some of the equipment he saw abroad.

Vocabulary:
aptitude = ability
au courant = up-to-date
eminent = distinguished
extruded = pushed out
  through a die
flambé = served flaming
  in liquor
reluctant = unwilling

Eli Whitney

The cotton gin

Almost everything we use today depends on mass production—the use of machines to turn out standardized parts at high speed and low cost. Our modern standard of living depends on this system; it would be impossible to return to the days of handcrafting the things we need and want.

The idea of replacing handcrafting with machines developed slowly. It became known as the "American System." The first steps in creating this system came from the inventive genius of Eli Whitney (1765-1825).

In a letter to his father, Whitney described how he invented the cotton gin, a machine that was to revolutionize cotton production.

Summary:
I heard how difficult it is to separate seed from cotton. I made a model of a little machine that might work.

Vocabulary:
expedition = a journey taken by a group of people with a specific purpose
guineas = a British gold coin worth one pound and one shilling

...I heard much said of the extreme difficulty of ginning cotton, that is, separating it from its seeds. There were a number of very respectable gentlemen at Mrs. Greene's who all agreed that if a machine could be invented which would clean the cotton with expedition, it would be a great thing both to the country and to the inventor. I involuntarily happened to be thinking on the subject and struck out a plan of a machine in my mind....

In about ten days I made a little model, for which I was offered, if I would give up all right and title to it, 100 guineas. I concluded to relinquish my school and turn my attention to perfecting the machine. I made one before I came away which required the labor of one man to turn it and with which one man will clean ten times as much cotton as he can in any other way before known, and also cleanse it much better than in the usual mode. This machine may be turned by water or with a horse with the greatest ease, and one man and a horse will do more than fifty men with the old machines. It makes the labor fifty times less, without throwing any class of people out of business....

How advantageous this business will eventually prove to me, I cannot say. It is generally said by those who know anything about it that I shall make my fortune by it. I have no expectation that I shall make an independent fortune by it, but I think I had better pursue it than any other business into which I can enter. Something which cannot be foreseen may frustrate my expectations and defeat my plan.... I wish you, sir, not to show this letter nor communicate anything of its contents to anybody except my brothers and sister, *enjoining* it on them to keep the whole a *profound secret*.

Source: C.M. Green, *Eli Whitney and the Birth of American Technology*. Boston: Little, Brown Co., 1956, p. 77.

Summary:
The new machine cleans the cotton much better than ever before. One worker can do as much as 50 men.

Some think I will make a fortune from this invention, but I'm not sure. I will pursue it and keep the plans secret.

Vocabulary:
advantageous = useful
enjoining = commanding
profound = absolute, complete
relinquish = abandon, put aside

The invention had the simplicity of genius. A box contained a cylinder with dozens of bent wires. The wires worked in slots wide enough for cotton fiber to pass through, but not the seeds. By turning a crank, hooks pulled the cotton through the slots, then a revolving wire brush completed the cleaning.

Whitney obtained a patent and set up a factory for producing cotton gins in New Haven, Connecticut, but he never made his fortune from it.

His early model was stolen and easily copied by others. Years of lawsuits followed and what money he did make was largely used up by lawyers' fees. His problems multiplied in 1795 when his factory burned to the ground.

He wrote of his miseries to fellow inventor Robert Fulton in 1811.

Vocabulary:
Cataract = a waterfall, or great downpour

...I have labored hard against the strong current of Disappointment which has been threatening to carry us down the Cataract of Destruction — but I have labored with a shattered oar and struggled in vain.

Source: C.M. Green, *Eli Whitney and the Birth of American Technology.* Boston: Little, Brown Co., 1956, p. 77.

In spite of the inventor's problems, cotton production soared from 4,000 bales in 1791 to 178,000 bales in 1810 and, by 1860, to more than 4,000,000 bales. The cotton fed mills in England and New England, where water-powered looms, invented in England, could turn out endless yards of cotton fabric. By the 1840s, 1200 American mills employed 70,000 workers.

Benjamin Banneker

Benjamin Banneker (1731-1806) grew up on his family's tobacco farm in Maryland. As a young man, he designed an irrigation system that allowed his family to grow tobacco, even when there was limited rainfall and other farmers' crops were failing all around the area. During the American Revolution, his system of irrigating crops allowed the troops to be supplied with wheat throughout the war, keeping them from starvation.

Banneker taught himself how to design watches and clocks, by taking apart a watch given to him by a friend. After studying the mechanism carefully, he was able to reproduce the parts on his own. He is credited with having made the first striking clock in America, and, based on his clock, is considered to be the first African American inventor. His genius flourished.

Banneker's curiosity was insatiable, and he went on to study astronomy from a cabin he built with a skylight, enabling him to lie on his back and look up at the stars. From this research, he published his first Almanac in 1792.

Vocabulary:
ephemeris = astronomical almanac
gratified = pleased

They [the publishers] feel gratified in the opportunity of presenting to the public through their press what must be considered as an extraordinary effort of genius—a complete and accurate ephemeris for the year 1792 calculated by an able son of Africa.

Source: *Catholic world*, vol. 38, iss. 225, Dec. 1883. Found on http://www.hti.umich.edu/cgi/m/moajrnl/

Brief examples of two keen observations described in his Almanacs follow.

December 23, 1790, about three o'clock, A.M., I heard the sound and felt the shock like heavy thunder, but could not observe any cloud above the horizon. I therefore conclude it must be a great earthquake in some part of the globe....

April 1800. The first great locust year that I can remember, was in 1749, I was then about 17 years of age, when thousands of them came and were creeping up the trees and bushes. I then imagined they came to eat and destroy the fruit of the earth, and would occasion a famine in the land; I therefore began to kill and destroy them, but soon saw that my labor was in vain. Again in 1766, which is 17 years from their first appearance, they made a second and full as numerous. I then had more sense than to destroy them, knowing they were not so pernicious. Again in the year 1783, which was 17 years from their second appearance to me, they made their third and they may be expected again in 1800.

Source: *Southern literary messenger;* vol. 23, iss.1, July 1856, "Bannaker, the Black Astronomer," Richmond, Virginia: T.W. White [etc.], pp. 65-7. Found on http://www.hti.umich.edu/cgi/m/moajrnl/

Consider this:
Summarize Banneker's notes in your own words.

Vocabulary:
pernicious = destructive; causing great harm

Thomas Jefferson, impressed with Banneker's ability, asked him to be on the committee to design the nation's new capital, in Washington, D.C. When the master designer, Pierre L'Enfant, was fired from the project, he angrily left with all of the plans. Banneker was able to recreate the plans for the layout of the city in only two days.

Farming Inventions of the 19th Century

John Deere

By the 1830s, farm families realized that new tools could increase production and profits. In the 1830s, John Deere (1804-1886) developed a plow with a steel blade. The steel made it possible for the first time to plow America's Great Plains, a vast area that had been known as the "Great American Desert," because it was believed that a plow could not cut through the thick sod.

With Deere's plow, farmers could now turn the entire prairie into wheat fields. First, however, they needed a way to harvest what they planted. Wheat ripens all at once; what cannot be harvested in the space of about two weeks is lost. A prairie farmer described the problem in 1839.

Consider this:
Can you think of a situation today where there is not enough "man-power" to get the work done? Describe it.

"You can behold the vast plain of 12,000 acres, all waving in golden color, ripe for the cradle. At this moment, every man and boy, and even women, are actively engaged in cradling, raking, binding, and shocking the golden harvest. ... But, after all, a large portion will be left out, and will be destroyed. There is not *help* enough in the country to secure the crop."

Source: Quoted in Marshall B. Davidson, *Life in America*, Vol. 1, Boston: Houghton Mifflin Company, 1951, p. 411.

The McCormick Reaper

The "help" came, not in the form of more workers, but in mechanizing the harvest. The pioneer in this agricultural revolution was Cyrus H. McCormick (1809-1884). McCormick conceived plans for a reaper in 1831, built and tested it, and then remodeled it for public trial, all within six weeks. On first viewing the reaper, the *Times* of London described it as:

Vocabulary:
contrivance = clever device
incomprehensible = incapable of being understood
unwieldy = clumsy

"...a cross between a flying machine, a wheelbarrow and an Astley chariot [a carriage] ...an extravagant Yankee contrivance, huge, unwieldy, unsightly and incomprehensible."

"The reaping machine from the United States is the most valuable contribution from abroad to the stock of our previous knowledge. ... It is worth the whole cost of the Exposition."

Source: The *Times* of London, 1851, quoted in Marshall B. Davidson, *Life in America,* vol. 1, Boston: Houghton Mifflin Company, 1951. p. 412.

American newspapers also extolled the virtues of McCormick's machine.

"The saucy machine has driven the scythe from the field, almost tempting old Time to choose a new weapon. Now the principal work of the harvest is to drive the horse about the field a few times and lo! the harvest is gathered."

Vocabulary:
saucy = disrespectful, impertinent

Source: *Philadelphia Photographer,* August, 1864.

The first reaper

The first reaper required two people to operate it: one to ride the horse and another to rake the cut grain from the platform. It cut as much grain in one day as four or five men with cradles or twelve men with reaping hooks. McCormick further refined his reaper, and finally took out a patent in 1834. Use of the reaper spread slowly at first, but soon it outpaced McCormick's ability to produce the machines at his blacksmith shop. In 1847, he moved to Chicago, where he marketed the reaper to the grain farmers of the Midwest. By the mid-1850s, the "Virginia Reaper" was a significant factor in westward expansion.

McCormick's enormous success was due in large part to his innovative business practices: easy credit terms, enabling farmers to pay for machines as their harvests increased; written guarantees, assuring farmers that the machine would work properly; and convincing advertising, that spread the word.

Joseph Glidden

Farming, ranching, and land management in the West were greatly influenced by the invention and subsequent widespread use of barbed wire. In a 20-year period, nine inventors submitted patents for wire fencing, but Joseph Glidden's design, patented in November 1874, was considered "the winner." Glidden's design not only included a method for locking the wire barbs in place, but he had developed the machinery to mass-produce the wire. It is still the most commonly used wire fencing today. Below is one of his patent application drawings and an excerpt from the patent application.

Consider This:
Make a list of some of the things that barbed wire fencing kept *in* and some of the things it kept *out*.

What effect did barbed wire fencing have on tribes of nomadic Indians? Explain.

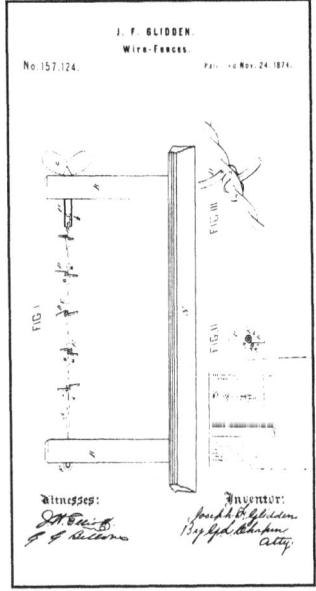

Wire-Fences. Patented by J.F. Glidden, Nov. 24, 1874.

UNITED STATES PATENT OFFICE
JOSEPH F. GLIDDEN, OF DE KALB, ILLINOIS.
IMPROVEMENT IN WIRE FENCES.

Specification forming part of letters Patent No.157124L dated Nov. 24, 1874; application filed Oct. 27, 1873.

To all whom it may concern:

Be it known that I, JOSEPH F. GLIDDEN, of De Kalb, in the county of De Kalb and State of Illinois, have invented a new and valuable Improvement in Wire Fences; and that the following is a full, clear, and exact description of the construction and operation of the same, reference being had to the accompanying drawings, in which—Figure I represents a side view of a section of fence exhibiting my invention. Fig. 2 is a sectional view, and Fig. 3 is a perspective view, of the same.

This invention [is] for preventing cattle from breaking through wire fences; and it consists in combining, with the twisted fence wires, a short transverse [crosswise] wire, coiled or bent at its central portion about one of the wire strands of the twist, with its free ends projecting in opposite directions, the other wire strand serving to bind the spur-wire firmly to its place and in position, with its spur ends perpendicular to the direction of the fence-wire, lateral [side-to-side] movement, as well as vibration, being prevented....

Source: National Archives and Records Administration, *Teaching with Documents*, Vol. 2, pp. 54-5.

George Washington Carver

George Washington Carver (1864-1943) was born into slavery in Missouri, and was raised by his owner, Moses Carver. Carver was educated, beginning at age 12, and soon developed a passion for studying plants.

In 1897, Booker T. Washington, founder of the Tuskegee Normal and Industrial Institute for Negroes, convinced Carver to come South and serve as the school's Director of Agriculture. It was at Tuskegee that Carver developed a crop-rotation method, which changed the practice of southern farming. Carver implemented a system for alternating soil-depleting cotton crops with soil-enriching crops which have nitrogen-fixing bacteria in their roots—such as peanuts, peas, soybeans, sweet potatoes, and pecans. Years of growing only cotton and tobacco had taken all of the nutrients from the soil. Carver convinced southern farmers to try his crop rotation method, which eventually changed the course of farming.

But, although the method enriched the soil for cotton and tobacco crops, farmers did not have much use for crops like peanuts, so Carver set to work to find new uses for the produce. He not only invented peanut butter, but more than three hundred other uses for peanuts, including cooking oil and printers' ink, and hundreds of uses for soybeans, pecans and sweet potatoes. Carver only patented three of his many inventions, because he believed "God gave them to me. How can I sell them to someone else?"

Some of the synthetic products developed by Carver include:

Adhesives	Mayonnaise	Synthetic Rubber	**Things to do:**
Axle Grease	Meal	Talcum Powder	Choose one of the
Bleach	Meat Tenderizer	Vanishing Cream	inventions that Carver
Buttermilk	Metal Polish	Wood Stains	worked on, and gather
Cheese	Milk Flakes	Wood Filler	information to share
Chili Sauce	Mucilage	Worcestershire	with the class.
Cream	Paper	Sauce	
Creosote	Rubbing Oils		
Dyes	Salve		
Flour	Soil Conditioner		
Fuel Briquettes	Shampoo		
Ink	Shoe Polish		
Instant Coffee	Shaving Cream		
Insulating Board	Sugar		
Linoleum	Synthetic Marble		

Source: Hattie Carwell, *Blacks in Science: Astrophysicist to Zoologist.* Hicksville, N.Y.: Exposition Press, 1977, p.18. Found at http://www. princeton.edu/~mcbrown/display/carver.html

Industrial Inventions of the 19th Century

Samuel Colt's Assembly Line

The next step in making mass production possible was the assembly line—having one worker complete one action, then pass the item along to the next person. The man most responsible for developing the assembly line was Samuel Colt (1814-1862), the man who invented the revolver, or six-shooter.

The combination of Whitney's interchangeable system and Colt's assembly line was soon applied to manufacturing dozens of products.

Colt turned to the Whitney Arms Company, now run by Eli Whitney, Jr. As profits grew, Colt built his own factory in Hartford, Connecticut, where he perfected the assembly line combined with Whitney's idea of interchangeable parts. In a letter to his father, he described how his system worked, with more than 400 machines in constant operation.

Consider this:
Although this method made the work go faster and the products become more standard, do you think the workers got bored doing the same task over and over again?

Vocabulary:
affix = attach

The first workman would receive two or three of the most important parts, and would affix these together and pass them on to the next who would do the same, and so on until the complete arm is put together. It would then be inspected and given the finishing touches by experts and each arm would be exactly alike and all of its parts would be the same. The workmen, by constant practice in a single operation would become highly skilled and at the same time very quick and expert at their particular task, so you have better guns and more of them for less money than if you hire men and have each one make the entire arm....

Source: Jack Rohan, *Yankee Arms Maker: The Incredible Career of Samuel Colt.* New York: Harper, 1935.

With hand labour it is not possible to obtain that amount of uniformity, or accuracy in the several parts, which is so desirable.... Nor could the quality required be produced by manual labor. ... There is nothing that cannot be produced by machiney.
— Samuel Colt, 1851.

Colt's American System proved itself in the 20th century, when America readied for war. During World War II, the machine gun factory pictured above was able to manufacture tens of thousands of guns each week, using Colt's method of interchangeable parts on an assembly line. (Library of Congress)

Morse and the Telegraph

Samuel F.B. Morse (1791-1872) was an artist, not an inventor. He knew almost nothing about electricity. And yet his invention of the telegraph had a more instantaneous impact on the shrinking of time and space than any other single invention.

Born in Massachusetts, Morse struggled for years as a portrait painter and landscape artist. Modern art historians consider him first-rate.

He decided to work on a telegraph machine, using electricity to send messages. When his simple model was completed, he shared his work with Joseph Henry (1797-1878), a brilliant scientist, who had already discovered the same ideas and helped Morse with advice. In fact, if Henry had bothered to patent his own ideas, he would have been credited with inventing the telegraph. The main new thing Morse contributed was his Morse Code *(see p. 54)*, using a series of dots and dashes for each letter in the alphabet.

Morse was ready to try his device, but he needed funds and turned to the government. In 1838, a Congressional report was enthusiastic.

Vocabulary:
annihilated = destroyed, wiped out

> It is obvious that the influence of this invention...will, in the event of success, of itself amount to a revolution unsurpassed in moral grandeur by any discovery that has been made in the arts and sciences.... Space will be, to all practical purposes of information, completely annihilated between the States of the Union.
>
> Source: E.L. Morse, ed., *Samuel F.B. Morse: His Letters and Journals.* Boston: Houghton Mifflin, 1914, p. 186.

Glowing praise—but no money. Not until 1843 did Congress provide $30,000 to construct a 30-mile telegraph line between Washington, D.C. and Baltimore. On May 24, 1844, Morse tapped out the historic first message, from Baltimore to the Supreme Court Building in Washington: "What hath God wrought!"

The result was a revolution in communication. Telegraph lines soon crisscrossed the nation. Messages that had once taken days or weeks to deliver, could now be transmitted in a matter of seconds. Perhaps the fastest means of communication before the telegraph became widely used was the Pony Express, organized in 1860, which could deliver mail 2,000 miles between St. Louis and San Francisco in just ten days. Morse's invention reduced the time to less than ten minutes.

Morse code caught on all over the world. This French operator is pictured at his telgraph machine. (French Government Tourist Office)

Although Morse eventually gained both fame and a considerable fortune, he first had to wage battles in court to uphold his patent. He finally won every lawsuit, but he was pained by the attacks on him.

I am held up by name to the odium of the public.... I find the fate of Whitney before me.... Take as much pains as you will to secure yourself, and your valuable invention, you will be robbed of it and abused in the bargain. This is the lot of the successful inventor and no precaution, I believe, will save him from it. ...the unprincipled will hate him and detract from his reputation to compass their own contemptible and selfish ends.	**Summary:** The public dislikes me, just as they did Eli Whitney. No matter how much you try to protect your invention, there will be those who try to steal it. **Vocabulary:** compass = scheme, plot contemptible = despicable odium = strong dislike
Source: E.L. Morse, ed., *Samuel F.B. Morse: His Letters and Journals*. Boston: Houghton Mifflin, 1914, p. 224.	

Elisha Otis: Conquering Vertical Space

Elisha G. Otis (1811-1861) invented a safety device which he demonstrated at New York's version of the Crystal Palace in 1854; after being hoisted to the top of the display, he dramatically ordered that the rope be cut. When the elevator didn't fall, his point was made. He formed the Otis Elevator Company and his sons later added electrical power to the elevators. This single invention made possible a revolution in architecture and construction. Taller buildings were now possible, and the first skyscrapers were soon under construction. A visitor to Chicago described the sensation of this vertical transportation.

Consider this:
How does the person's language give you the impression of an elevator ride—both up and down?

"The slow-going stranger…feels himself loaded into one of those…baskets…and the next instant up goes the whole load as a feather caught up by a gale. The descent is more simple. Something lets go, and you fall from ten to twenty stories as it happens."

Source: Quoted in Bessie Louise Pierce, ed., *As Others See Chicago*. Chicago, 1933.

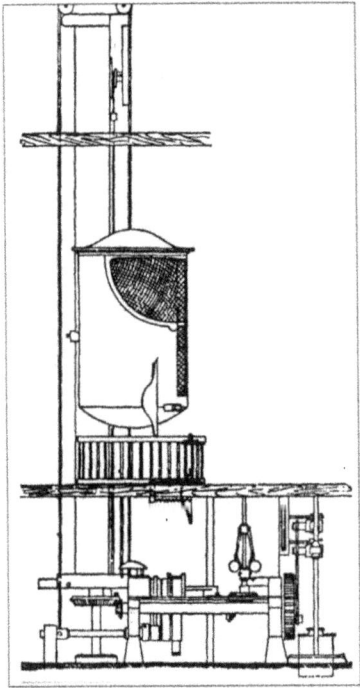

William Ellery Hale made a fortune with his early passenger elevator.

In 1852, Otis' "safety elevator" had a catch, to prevent the car from falling.

The Inventive Spirit Takes Hold

The U. S. Patent Office issued 5,942 patents during the 1840s, and 23,140 in the 1850s. Between 1870 and 1900, the U. S. Patent Office issued 640,000 new patents. While the patents included such wonders as the telephone and electric light, most of the inventors of these patents made no fortunes and gained no lasting fame. But they kept right on inventing, motivated by that American notion that there must be a faster or better way of doing everything.

> "Why I could make anything a body wanted—it didn't make any difference what; and if there wasn't any quick new fangled way to make a thing, I could invent one—and do it as easy as falling off a log...."

Source: Mark Twain, *A Connecticut Yankee in King Arthur's Court*, 1889.

Historian Bernard A. Weisberger described the achievements of the inventors between 1875 and 1900:

> They set the gloom of night aglow with cheery electric light, enabled the people in all corners of the land to talk to one another. They made machines that talked, cameras a child could work, typewriters, barbed wire and workable safety pins. As they produced their marvels, the soldiers and statesmen, the nation's heroes for two-thirds of the century, faded away. Now the heroes were the inventors—Thomas Alva Edison, Alexander Graham Bell, John Augustus Roebling, George Eastman, George Westinghouse.... They built a new civilization, based on machines and mass production.

Source: Bernard A. Weisberger, *The LIFE History of the U.S., Vol. 7, The Age of Steel and Steam*. NY: Time, Inc., 1964, p. 38.

Consider this:

Which one invention do you think was most significant, and why?

What did Roebling, Eastman, and Westinghouse invent?

During this period, inventors replaced soldiers and statesmen as heroes. Who are our heroes today?

Bell's Telephone

In 1876, the United States celebrated the nation's Centennial with a magnificent Centennial Exhibition in Philadelphia. One of the smallest displays in any of the buildings was a table containing Alexander Graham Bell's telephone, which the inventor had patented a few weeks before the Exhibition opened. Only a few of the eight million visitors paid much attention to the strange-looking device. Fewer still suspected how important this invention was to become.

Scottish-born Alexander Graham Bell (1847-1922) was, like his father, a teacher of the deaf. After migrating to Canada, then to the United States, he became increasingly interested in the idea of reproducing sound. The Western Union Telegraph Company, which by now had strung some 400,000 miles of telegraph wires, was looking for a way to send several telegraph messages over the same wire at the same time. The prize offered was a good incentive to young inventors like Bell. "If I can make the deaf talk," he declared, "I can make iron talk."

Consider this:
Bell's attitude was shaped by Morse and Henry. Explain how.

Vocabulary:
laconic = concise, terse

Bell's letter to his parents

It would be possible to transmit sounds of ANY SORT if we could [create] a variation in the intensity of an electric current like that occurring in the density of air....

My inexperience in such matters is a great drawback. However, Morse conquered his electrical difficulties even though he was only a painter, and I have no intention of giving in either....

[Joseph Henry] said he thought it was "the germ of a great invention"....I said I recognized that there were mechanical difficulties....I added that I felt that I had not the electrical knowledge necessary to overcome the difficulties. His laconic answer was "Get it." I cannot tell you how much those two words encouraged me.

Source: R.V. Bruce, *Alexander Graham Bell and the Conquest of Solitude*. London: Gollancz Co., 1973.

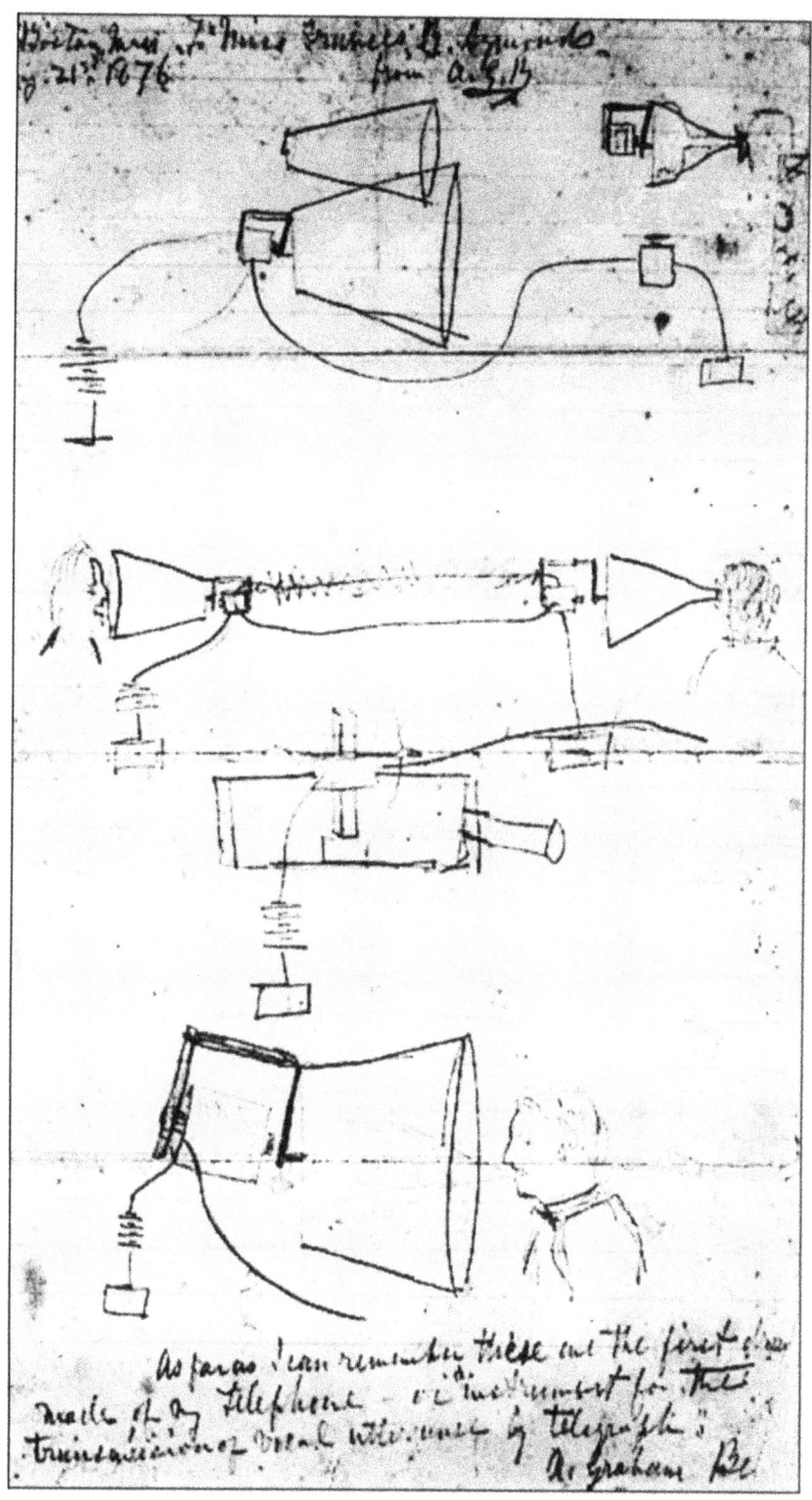

Bell's design sketch of the telephone, around 1876. (Library of Congress)

Bell's first telephone

Reactions to what Bell called the telephone were mixed. Here is a sampling.

Consider this:
It's hard for us to imagine how different life would be today, without the telephone.

Make a list of at least 10 ways that it would affect your life.

The Centennial Exhibition has afforded the opportunity to bring into public view many inventions and improvements which otherwise would only have been known to the smaller circles.... The tele-phone is a curious device that might fairly find place in the magic of Arabian Tales. Of what use is such an invention? Well, there may be occasions of state when it is necessary for officials who are far apart to talk with each other without the interference of a [telegraph] operator. Or some lover might wish to pop the question directly into the ear of a lady and hear for himself her reply, though miles away; it is not for us to guess how courtships will be carried on in the Twentieth Century....

Source: New York *Tribune*, Nov. 4, 1876.

With my ear pressed against a disc, I heard it speak distinctly several sentences...I need scarcely say I was astonished and delighted. ...With somewhat more advanced plans, and more powerful apparatus, we may confidently expect that Mr. Bell will give us the means of making voice and spoken words audible through the electric wire to an ear hundreds of miles distant.

Source: Scottish scientist Sir William Thomson, quoted in Bruce Norman, *The Inventing of America,* NY: Taplinger Publishing Company, 1976, p. 56.

The latest American humbug—far inferior to the well-established speaking tubes....

Source: *The Times of London,* July, 1876.

Western Union agreed with *The Times*. When Bell offered to sell his invention for $100,000, the company president turned him down, saying, "What use can we make of an electrical toy?"

Bell, with financial backing from his father-in-law, started his own company. Thomas Alva Edison contributed a key component to the improved telephone by inventing a transmitter using a carbon button, not much different from the transmitter on modern telephones. Western Union bought Edison's transmitter and hired him to compete with Bell, clearly infringing on Bell's patent, while the Bell Telephone Company freely used Edison's transmitter. Other inventors, including Elisha Gray and Emile Berliner, became involved and years of court wrangling followed—a total of some 600 lawsuits.

The legal battles didn't prevent Edison from gaining a profit and having fun, while Bell deservedly earned a considerable fortune and immense popularity. And the early derision of the telephone did not interfere with its amazing growth. By 1880, only four years after Bell's patent was granted, there were 50,000 telephones in operation, Within twenty years, there were more than one million. Bell, now a wealthy man at the age of thirty, left the business in 1881 and returned to teaching the deaf.

Thomas Alva Edison

The Phonograph

Edison made his first recording, "Mary had a little lamb," on this phonograph. (National Archives)

Edison described how working on the transmitter for Bell's telephone led him to the idea of a phonograph.

Things to do:
Find out some other major inventions which were discovered as a result of an accident.

I discovered the principle by the merest accident. I was singing to the mouthpiece of a telephone when the vibrations of the voice sent the fine steel point into my finger. That set me thinking. If I could record the actions of the point and send the point over some surface afterward, I saw no reason why the thing would not talk. I tried the experiment first on a string of telegraph paper [waxed strips about half an inch wide] and found that the point made an alphabet [i.e., marked the paper with tiny holes]. I shouted the words "Hallo! Hallo!" into the mouthpiece, ran the paper back over the steel point and heard a faint "Hallo! Hallo!" in return. I determined to make a machine that would work accurately and gave my assistants instructions, telling them what I had discovered. That's the whole story. The phonograph is the result of the pricking of a finger.

Source: W.K. Dickson, *The Life and Inventions of Thomas Alva Edison*. London: Chatto & Windus, 1894, p. 122.

Electric Lighting

One reason Edison had stopped work on the phonograph was a sudden new passion—electric lights. Edison did not invent electric lighting. By 1878, several cities in Europe and the U. S. were partially illuminated by "arc lights" —a current of electricity flowing between two carbonized poles or rods. Arc lights used such a huge amount of electricity and produced such a brilliant light that they could only be used for street lighting. The problem was that the electrical current could not be subdivided into smaller units that could be used in homes and businesses. A British government report in 1878 stated emphatically: "The sub-division of the electric light is a problem that cannot be solved by the human brain."

To solve the problem, several inventors were trying to create a "glow lamp" —a lamp in which electric current caused a rod, or filament, to glow without burning up. This is *incandescent* light, and this was Edison's great triumph. This is how Edison described the problem.

To the question: "Which invention caused you the most study? Thomas Edison replied... The electric light. For, although I was never myself discouraged, or inclined to be hopeless of success, I cannot say the same for all of my associates. And yet, through all those years of experimenting and research, I never once made a discovery. All my work was deductive, and the results I achieved were those of invention pure and simple. I would construct a theory and work on its lines until I found it was untenable. Then it would be discarded at once, and another theory evolved. This was the only possible way for me to work out the problem, for the conditions under which the incandescent electric light exists are peculiar and unsatisfactory for close investigation. Just consider this: we have an almost infinitesmal filament heated to a degree which it is difficult for us to comprehend, and it is in a vacuum, under conditions of which we are wholly ignorant. You cannot use your eyes

(continued on next page)

Consider this:
Summarize this excerpt in your own words.

Vocabulary:
deductive = drawing conclusions from reasoning
comprehend = understand
untenable = not defendable

> to help you in the investigation, and you really know nothing of what is going on in that tiny bulb. I speak without exaggeration when I say that I have constructed *three thousand* different theories in connection with the electric light, each one of them reasonable and apparently likely to be true. Yet in only two cases did my experiments prove the truth of my theory.
>
> Source: George Parsons Lathrop, "Talks With Edison," *Harper's Magazine*, LXXX, Feb., 1909.

After months of effort, Edison found that carbonized bamboo created a long-lasting filament, and he had his incandescent light bulb. Bamboo remained the standard filament until the modern tungsten filament was developed a few years later.

Edison turned next to what was probably his greatest achievement—creating an entire system to deliver electric lighting to customers. This meant devising generators to produce the electrical current, an underground system of wiring to carry the current to homes and businesses, meters to measure the amount of electricity used, as well as switches for lamps and sockets to hold the bulbs. It took nearly three years to develop all these components and to build the first power station in New York City.

Even after the power station was opened, many observers remained convinced that electric lights would not replace gas light. As late as 1895, *Popular Science* magazine concluded:

Things to do:
Find a review in a fairly recent technology or science journal that you think might be proven wrong in the future, and explain why you think so.

> Not withstanding the rapid development of electric lighting, the use of gas in dwelling houses, offices, and stores is undoubtedly so convenient and comparatively safe that for many years it will remain the chief means of artificial illumination.
>
> Source: *Popular Science*, quoted in Ernest V. Heyn, *Fire of Genius: Inventors of the Past Century.* NY: Doubleday, 1976, p. 135.
>
> **Note:** More details and stories of Edison's life and work are available in David C. King's book, *Thomas Alva Edison: The King of Inventors,* Carlisle, MA: Discovery Enterprises, Ltd., 1995.

Motion Pictures

In the late 1880s, Edison turned his attention to what would be his last great series of inventions—the basic apparatus for motion pictures.

What primarily interested me in motion pictures [was] the hope of developing something that would do for the eye what the phonograph did for the ear. That was the broad purpose, but how to accomplish that purpose was a problem which seemed more impossible the longer I studied it. It was in 1887 that I began my investigations.... The experiments in a laboratory consist mostly of finding that something won't work. The worst of it is you never know beforehand and sometimes it takes months, even years, before you discover you had been wrong all the time....

Source: Dagobert D. Runes, ed., *The Diary and Sundry Observations of Thomas Alva Edison*. NY: The Philosophical Library, Inc., 1948.

Consider this:
Explain what Edison meant by "The experiments in a laboratory consist mostly of finding that something won't work." Give some concrete examples from your research.

Edison finally succeeded in developing a workable motion picture camera, the kinetograph.

[Our first pictures] were shown...in an apparatus we christened "The Kinetescope," consisting of a cabinet equipped with an electrical motor and battery, and carrying a fifty-foot band of film, passed through the field of a magnifying glass. They attracted quite a lot of attention at the World's Fair in Chicago in 1893....

As in the case of the phonograph, Edison failed to see the potential of motion pictures. He decided against developing a projector and movie screen, saying that too many people could see a film at the same time and they would soon lose interest.

Lewis Howard Latimer

Lewis Howard Latimer (1848-1928) worked with Thomas Edison for many years and was credited with a number of inventons, including an improved filament for light bulbs and an improved socket. Although he received little acclaim during his lifetime, when he died in 1928, the *Edison Pioneers* (members of the early group who had worked with Edison) offered these words on Latimer.

Consider this:

Latimer was extremely talented and very productive, yet he got little credit for his inventions in his lifetime. How much of that was due to his race? Would an obituary today mention someone's race?

...In this office he became interested in draughting and gradually perfected himself to such a degree as to become their chief draughtsman.... It was Mr. Latimer who executed the drawings and assisted in preparing the applications for the telephone patents of Alexander Graham Bell. In 1880 he entered the employ of Hiram S. Maxim, Electrician of the United States Electric Lighting Co., then located at Bridgeport, Connecticut. It was while in this employ that Mr. Latimer successfully produced a method of making carbon filaments for the Maxim electric incandescent lamp, which he patented. His keen perception of the possibilities of the electric light and kindred industries resulted in his being the author of several other inventions.... In 1884 he became associated with the Engineering Department of the Edison Electric Light Company.

He was of the colored race, the only one in our organization, and was one of those to respond to the initial call that led to the formation of the Edison Pioneers, January 24,1918. Broadmindedness, versatility in the accomplishment of things intellectual and cultural, a linguist, a devoted husband and father, all were characteristic of him, and his genial presence will be missed from our gatherings.

Source: William Loren Katz, *Eyewitness: A Living Documentary of the African American Contribution to American History.* New York: Simon & Schuster, Touchstone Edition, 1995.

Life-Altering Inventions of the 20th Century

Henry Ford

In 1899, there were only about fifty automobiles in the entire country, and inventors had been tinkering with them for more than twenty years. A number of thorny problems had to be worked out, including how to make a small engine with a portable and efficient fuel supply and devising systems for starting, stopping, and steering the vehicle. Following ideas developed in Europe, the Duryea brothers of Springfield, MA, developed what is regarded as the first American automobile in 1891, and later actually built twelve more. Not far behind was one of Edison's employees working in Detroit, a young mechanic named Henry Ford (1863-1947). By 1893, Ford had designed and built his first car, the "Quadricycle."

Henry Ford in his Quadricycle (Library of Congress)

Perhaps no single individual had a greater impact on American life in the 1920s than Henry Ford. He revolutionized the automobile industry by making his Model Ts—the famous "Tin Lizzies" —affordable for the average family. In the process, Ford preached a lesson that business people did not forget: mass production leads to lower costs which leads to mass consumption.

Ford explained it this way:

Summary:
The commodities that make life more comfortable can only be afforded by a few [wealthy] people. Ford Motor Company can produce cars inexpensively for the masses. If production is increased, then costs are lowered, and many more people will be able to buy cars.

Vocabulary:
conduce = contribute to a result

The commodities that conduce to civilized living are thus far enjoyed by only a small fraction of the world's inhabitants. The experience of the Ford Motor Company has been that mass production precedes mass consumption and makes it possible by reducing costs.... If the production is increased 500 percent, costs may be cut 50 percent, and the decrease in cost, with its accompanying decrease in selling price, will probably multiply by 10 the number of people who can conveniently buy the product. This is a conservative illustration of production serving as the cause of demand instead of the effect.

Source: Henry Ford, quoted in Marshall B. Davidson, *Life in America*. Boston: Houghton Mifflin Co., 1951, Vol. II, p. 284.

Ford's ideas worked remarkably well. The price of a Model T, which had first sold for $825 in 1910, dropped to $290 by 1924. He also introduced installment buying, so one of his "flivvers" [a cheap car] could be purchased for as little as $25 down. By 1920, there were eight million automobiles in America, and that number doubled over the next six years. Not surprisingly, one out of every five cars was a Model T.

Consider this:
Take another invention from the late 20th century, and describe how newer versions have improved it.

[My] first car had something of the appearance of a buggy.... The power was transmitted from the motor to the countershaft by a belt and from the countershaft to the rear wheel by a chain.... There were two speeds—one of ten and the other of twenty miles per hour—obtained by shifting the belt, which was done by a clutch lever in front of the driving seat.... There was no reverse.... The wheels were 28-inch bicycle wheels with rubber tires....

My "gasoline buggy" was the first and for a long time the only automobile in Detroit. It was considered to be something of a nuisance, for it made a racket and scared horses. Also it

"Tin Lizzies" were soon causing traffic jams across the nation. (Library of Congress)

blocked [horse-drawn] traffic. For if I stopped my machine anywhere in town a crowd was around it before I could start it up again. If I left it alone even for a minute some inquisitive person always tried to run it. Finally, I had to carry a chain and chain it to a lamp post whenever I left it anywhere.

Source: Henry Ford, *My Life and Work*. New York: Doubleday, Page & Co., 1922, pp. 32-3.

It was not until 1908 that Ford worked out a system for producing automobiles. By combining Whitney's system of interchangeable parts with Colt's assembly line, he was able to speed up production and lower costs. It was Ford's innovations that popularized the automobile by making it affordable. Ford's Model T stayed in production for twenty years and more than 15 million of the "Tin Lizzies" were sold—one out of every three cars on the road.

The Wright Brothers

Human flight had been dreamed of for centuries. Orville (1871-1948) and Wilbur Wright (1867-1912) achieved the first powered, sustained, and controlled flight of an airplane. In 1893, the brothers opened a bicycle shop to support their experiments in flight. After studying all available material on the subject, Wilbur built a five-foot model biplane in 1899, which he flew like a kite. The brothers had been fascinated with flight since childhood, as this recollection, written in 1908, explains.

Vocabulary:
abiding = enduring, lasting
sublime = awe inspiring
torsion = being twisted or turned

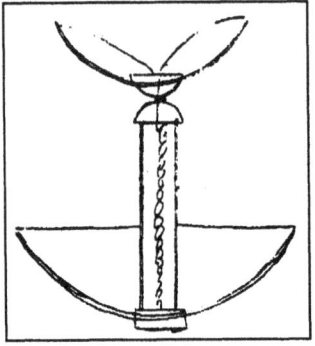

Orville Wright's drawing of the helicopter. (Found on http://www.first-to-fly.com/History/biograph.htm)

Late in the autumn of 1878, our father came into the house one evening with some object partly concealed in his hands, and before we could see what it was, he tossed it into the air. Instead of falling to the floor, as we expected, it flew across the room till it struck the ceiling, where it fluttered awhile, and finally sank to the floor. It was a little toy, known to scientists as a "helicoptere," but which we, with sublime disregard for science, at once dubbed a "bat." It was a light frame of cork and bamboo, covered with paper, which formed two screws, driven in opposite directions by rubber bands under torsion. A toy so delicate lasted only a short time in the hands of small boys, but its memory was abiding.

Source: Orville and Wilbur Wright, "The Wright Brothers Aeroplane," *Century Magazine*, September, 1908; in the Digital Library of the Invention of the Airplane.

The brothers built and tested a full-scale glider in 1900. A second glider followed two years later. Based on the experience of thousands of glider runs and experiments in a homemade wind tunnel, the brothers compiled new, more accurate data on the effects of wing design on lift, drag, and center of pressure. Using a system of rudders and wing deformation, they created a balanced aircraft that could be controlled by the pilot on all three axes of rotation. In practical terms, it was the first airplane that could safely and predictably move up or down, left or right. The only thing left to do was to add an engine. They completed their first powered machine, the Kitty Hawk, in 1903, and made history's first powered, sustained, and controlled airplane flights from level ground without any assistance at takeoff on the morning of December 17, 1903.

The first flight, with Orville as pilot, traveled 120 feet in twelve seconds. Later, Wilbur extended the flight time to fifty-nine seconds before a gust of wind flipped the aircraft, making it unable to fly. Their own account of that eventful day continues from their 1908 article.

...The first flights with the power-machine were made on the 17th of December, 1903. Only five persons besides ourselves were present. ...Although a general invitation had been extended to the people living within five or six miles, not many were willing to face the rigors of a cold December wind in order to see, as they no doubt thought, another flying-machine not fly. The first flight lasted only twelve seconds, a flight very modest compared with that of birds, but it was, nevertheless, the first in the history of the world in which a machine carrying a man had raised itself by its own power into the air in free flight, had sailed forward on a level course without reduction of speed, and had finally landed without being wrecked. The second and third flights were a little longer, and the fourth lasted fifty-nine seconds, covering a distance of 852 feet over the ground against a twenty-mile wind.

After the last flight, the machine was carried back to camp and set down in what was thought to be a safe place. But a few minutes later, while we were engaged in conversation about the flights, a sudden gust of wind struck the machine, and started to turn it over. All made a rush to stop it, but we were too late. Mr. Daniels, a giant in stature and strength, was lifted off his feet, and falling inside, between the surfaces, was shaken about like a rattle in a box as the machine rolled over and over. He finally fell out upon the sand with nothing worse than painful bruises, but the damage to the machine caused a discontinuance of experiments.

Summary:
We made the first flights with very few people in attendance. We had invited people who lived nearby, but they thought the flight would not be successful. The first flight was very short, but the plane flew on its own power, stayed level, and landed without crashing. The second, third, and fourth flights were longer.

After the last flight, a gust of wind blew the plane over and damaged it, so we had to discontinue the tests.

Wilbur Wright in 1901 glider flight. (Library of Congress)

The idea of powered flight was slow to catch on, but the Wrights kept working to improve their design. After much doubt from the public and skeptical reviews from *Scientific American,* the Wright brothers conducted several successful exhibition flights in New York and France. Business began to boom at their new American Wright Company. The Wrights became increasingly well-known, and they described their work in the 1908 article quoted earlier. In the following excerpt, they vividly conveyed the feeling of flying in their machine.

Consider this:

Summarize this passage in your own words.

You take your seat at the center of the machine beside the operator. He slips the cable, and you shoot forward. An assistant who has been holding the machine in balance on the rail, starts forward with you, but before you have gone fifty feet the speed is too great for him, and he lets go. Before reaching the end of the track the operator moves the front rudder, and the machine lifts from the rail like a kite supported by the pressure of the air underneath it. The ground under you is at first a perfect blur, but as you rise the objects become clearer. At a height of one hundred feet you feel hardly any motion at all, except for the wind which strikes your face. If you did not take the precaution to fasten your hat before starting, you have probably lost it by this time. The operator moves a lever: the right wing rises, and the machine swings about to the left. You make a very short turn, yet you do not feel the sensation of being thrown from your seat, so often experienced in automobile and railway travel. You find yourself facing toward the point from which you started. The objects on the ground now seem to be moving at much higher speed, though you perceive no change in the pressure of the wind on your face. You know then that you are traveling with the wind. When you near the starting point, the operator stops the motor while still high in the air. The machine coasts down at an oblique angle to the ground, and after sliding fifty or a hundred feet comes to rest. Although the machine often lands when traveling at a speed of a mile a minute, you feel no shock whatever, and cannot, in fact, tell the exact moment at which it first touched the ground. The motor close beside you kept up an almost deafening roar during the whole flight, yet in your excitement, you did not notice it till it stopped.

Vocabulary:
oblique = slanting angle, not parallel or perpendicular

On May 23 1906 the United States granted Patent Number 821,393 to O. & W. Wright of Dayton, Ohio for a Flying Machine. This would come to be considered the "grandfather patent" of the airplane.

Source: Found on http://www.first-to-fly.com/History/politics.htm)

The first flight on December 17, 1903, with Orville at the controls.
(Library of Congress)

The Computer Age

Herman Hollerith
The Electric Sorting and Tabulating Machine

Modern data processing began with the inventions of American engineer Herman Hollerith (1860-1929), who sought to develop a mechanized method for counting the nation's census data. Tabulating the 1880 census had taken the United States Census Bureau eight years to complete, and federal officials feared that the 1890 census would take even longer. In 1881, Hollerith began designing a machine to compile census data more efficiently than traditional hand methods, and by the late 1880s, he had built a punched card tabulating machine that could be read by electrical sensing. His system made it possible for one Census Bureau employee to compute each day the data on thousands of people, keypunching information that had been captured by tens of thousands of census takers.

The…Pantograph Punch…sped the transfer of data from the census taker's sheet to a punched card. When a stylus was inserted into a hole on the template, a corresponding hole was punched in the card at the other end. Each card represented one person and each hole a different statistic, such as age or marital status. The cards were sorted and later read electronically by a press containing pins that penetrated the card only at its holes. Each pin that passed through a hole made electrical contact with a small cup of mercury, closing a circuit and advancing a dial counter by one. Hollerith's machines completed the 1890 census in one year, garnering considerable publicity and leading to the establishment of his own company, the Tabulating Machine Company, which later became International Business Machines Corporation (IBM). For decades, Hollerith's punched card system was used in a variety of industries, most notably by IBM to program its early computers.

Source: Leonard C. Bruno, Manuscript Division, Library of Congress, Herman Hollerith Papers.

Many references state that Hollerith originally made his punched cards the same size as the dollar bills of that era, because he realized that it would be convenient and economical to buy existing office furniture, such as desks and cabinets, that already contained receptacles to accommodate stacks of bills. Other sources consider this to be a popular fiction. Whatever the case, we do know that these cards were eventually standardized at 7 and 3/8 inches by 3 and 1/4 inches, and Hollerith's many patents permitted his company (which became International Business Machines (IBM) in 1924) to hold an effective monopoly on punched cards for many years.

Source: Copyright (c) 1997, Maxfield & Montrose Interactive Inc. Found on http://www.maxmon.com/punch1.htm

Herman Hollerith's electrical tabulator was invented in the 1880s. From punched cards, the machine recorded data by moving the pointers on the dials. When the census was tabulated in 1880, the process took almost eight years to complete by hand. By 1890, the punch card system with the tabulator brought the work time for computing the results of the census down to a year. (IBM)

Grace Hopper

Grace Murray Hopper (1906-1992) was one of the key forces in making computers accessible to the average person. Her inventions focused on computer languages, which actually "taught computers to understand English," instead of just recognizing binary codes (which used only 1s and 0s). Binary codes made it easy to make mistakes and very difficult to find them.

Consider this:
What would your life be like today without computers?

Vocabulary:
computer compiler = a computer program that translates an entire set of instructions written in a higher-level symbolic language into machine language before the instructions can be executed. Source: Merriam Websters Online Dictionary.

In 1952, she developed the first computer compiler for the UNIVAC computer. Initially it was called the B-O compiler and then later renamed FLOW-MATIC. The compiler worked like a form of shorthand that called up the code already written in the computer files. This allowed for computers to be used for normal business operations like automated billing and payroll calculation. By the end of 1956 she had reached her goal of "teaching" UNIVAC I and II to recognize English statements.

In 1959, she took her work one step further and invented the computer language COBOL, the first user-friendly business software program. She worked hard to get this standardized and soon the Navy and others were using the language.

Her work has changed the face of computing. She was the first person ever to receive the Computer Sciences Man of the Year Award from the Data Processing Management Association in 1969. In 1991, she was the first individual woman to receive the National Medal of Technology. The Navy has celebrated her accomplishments by naming one their newest destroyers in her honor, the *U.S.S. Hopper.*

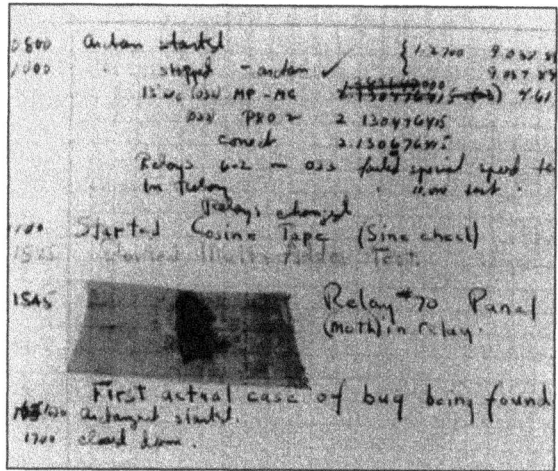

First actual case of bug being found. (Found on http://www.history.navy.mil/photos)

Computer bugs

[Grace Hopper] was the first person to coin this term when she found a moth jammed into a computer processor had stopped its operation. [On 09 Sep. 1945 they removed a moth from Relay #70, Panel F, of the Harvard University Mark II Aiken Relay Calculator.

The operators affixed the moth to the computer log, with the entry: "First actual case of bug being found." They put out the word that they had "debugged" the machine, thus introducing the term "debugging a computer program."

In 1988, the log, with the moth still taped by the entry, was in the Naval Surface Warfare Center Computer Museum at Dahlgren, Virginia.]

Source: Found on http://www.inventorsmuseum.com/GraceHopper.htm. Used with permission of the Inventors Museum.

Consider this:
Did you think that a "computer bug" was originally a real bug? What does the term refer to today?

Grace Hopper challenged all of us with this message: "A ship in port is safe, but that is not what ships are for. Sail out to sea and do new things."

Robotics

You've all heard of robots, but you may not be aware of all of the research and experimentation that is currently underway in this rapidly growing field. Encarta defines the robot as:

"[A] computer-controlled machine that is programmed to move, manipulate objects, and accomplish work while interacting with its environment. Robots are able to perform repetitive tasks more quickly, cheaply, and accurately than humans.

"...In 1995, about 700,000 robots were operating in the industrialized world. Over 500,000 were used in Japan, about 120,000 in Western Europe, and about 60,000 in the United States. Many robot applications are for tasks that are either dangerous or unpleasant for human beings.

"...In medical laboratories, robots handle potentially hazardous materials, such as blood or urine samples. In other cases, robots are used in repetitive, monotonous tasks in which human performance might degrade over time. Robots can perform these repetitive, high-precision operations 24 hours a day without fatigue.

"...Robots are being used to assist surgeons in installing artificial hips, and very high-precision robots can assist surgeons with delicate operations on the human eye. Research in telesurgery uses robots, under the remote control of expert surgeons that may one day perform operations in distant battlefields."

Source: "Robot," Microsoft® Encarta® Online Encyclopedia 2000 http:encarta.msn.com © 1997-2000 Microsoft Corporation. Contributed by George A. Bekey, B.S., M.S., Ph.D. Gordon Marshall Professor of Computer Science and Director of the Robotics Research Laboratory, University of Southern California.

How Robotic Surgery Will Work
by Kevin Bonsor

Just as computers revolutionized the latter half of the 20th century, the field of robotics has the potential to equally alter how we live in the 21st century. We've already seen how robots have changed the manufacturing of cars and other consumer goods by streamlining and speeding up the assembly line. We even have robotic lawn mowers and robotic pets now. And robots have enabled us to see places that humans are not yet able to visit, such as other planets and the depths of the ocean.

In the coming decades, we will see robots that have artificial intelligence, coming to resemble the humans that create them. They will eventually become self-aware and conscious, and be able to do anything that a human can. When we talk about robots doing the tasks of humans, we often talk about the future, but the future of robotic surgery is already here. Are we really ready for machines to take the place of human doctors in the operating room?

The first generation of surgical robots are already being installed in a number of operating rooms around the world. These aren't true autonomous robots that can perform surgical tasks on their own, but they are lending a mechanical helping hand to surgeons. These machines will still require a human surgeon to operate them and input instructions. Remote control and voice activation are the methods by which these surgical robots are controlled.

Robotics are being introduced to medicine because they allow for unprecedented control and precision of surgical instruments in minimally invasive procedures. So far, these machines have been used to position an endoscope, perform gallbladder surgery and correct gastroesophogeal reflux and heartburn. The ultimate goal of the robotic surgery field is to design a robot that can be used to perform closed-chest, beating-heart surgery. According to one manufacturer, robotic devices could be used in more than 3.5 million medical procedures per year in the United States alone.

Source: Kevin Bonsor, found at website http://www.howstuffworks.com/roboticsurgery.htm

Vocabulary:
autonomous = independent, self-contained
endoscope = an instrument for examining the inside of a body canal or hollow organ
gastroesophogeal reflux = flowing back from the stomach to the esophagus
invasive = tending to invade healthy tissue
unprecedented = not seen in the past

And, they still keep coming up with new ideas...

There will always be inventors and inventions. Almost every day, some newspaper article or electronic media source reports on some of the latest technology. Following are a few short clips from some of the thousands of new projects recently come to light.

Consider this:

How do you think these work?

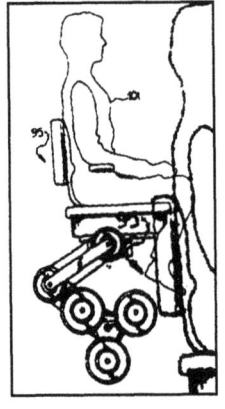

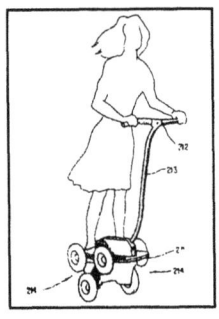

Dean Kamen

Dean Kamen of DEKA Research and Development Corp. is a young, very successful inventor and entrepreneur, living and working in New Hampshire. As of this writing, he holds 96 patents, two of which are described below:

Human Transporter:

For a motorized wheelchair that can climb curbs and even stairs. Kamen has developed such a chair, the Independent 3000 IBOT Transporter, which is scheduled for availability in mid-2002. Patent No. 5,701965 Dec. 30, 1997.

Transportation Vehicles and Methods:

For a motorized, one-passenger vehicle that looks like a vacuum cleaner crossed with a scooter. This drawing has been the center of some speculation surrounding project "Ginger." Patent No. 5,971,091 Oct. 26, 1999.

Source: Nathan Cobb, "Mystery Science 2001," *The Boston Globe*, February 1, 2001, p. C6.

In times past, inventors either funded their research themselves, or solicited a few investors who believed in their projects and wanted to participate in the development of their new inventions.

The inventions were often demonstrated at National and International Expositions and World Fairs, where the press would review them. Sometimes the critics could spot a winner in a flash, and sometimes they were totally wrong about the potential of a new device.

In today's world of the internet and numerous technology magazines and journals, the word on new products can be spread to millions of people everywhere, with very little effort. Some venture capital companies lend money to individuals or companies that are trying to develop and market new technology.

Following, is a typical listing of new electronics devices at a recent trade show.

Digital Devices Unveiled at Consumer Show

January 8, 2001

By May Wong, Las Vegas

...Vendors spread out a plethora of new consumer products—some useful, some amusing—over more than 1.2 million square feet of exhibit space at the trade show.

Here's a sampling of wares American consumers can expect this year:

Ultra fancy wristwear: Samsung's Watch Phone tells time, saves voice memos and is a mobile cellphone that can be dialed by voice command. A new Casio wrist watch is touted as the first wearable digital camera and holds up to 100 images.

A growing crop of Web appliances: devices designed either to fit under a kitchen counter or be toted around the home provide wireless Internet access away from a clunky desktop computer. One fancy offering will be Sony's Airboard, a touch-screen tablet allowing users wireless access to the Web and e-mail while they watch TV from almost anywhere inside their homes.

The Truster: a small, portable lie detector that uses voice recognition technology to sense when a person is telling a lie.

A digital French skillet by Digital Cookware, Inc. The display on the pan handle beeps to alert the cook when the pan's target temperature has been reached. A digital recipe book is included.

Consider this:
Which of these electronic devices do you think will be popular, and why?

Some inventions are very important for the way we live. Others are products or methods that save money, time, or just make our lives easier. How would you classify the products described here?

Vocabulary:
plethora = an excess
touted = publicized as having great worth

With new technology changing by the minute, the future holds the answers to many new developments that will be commonplace in your lifetime. Perhaps, you'll be one of the great American inventors included in a little volume such as this in the year 2050.

Research Activities/Things to Do

- The spirit of invention was contagious. One good idea led to another, and inventors often shared their ideas and technology to work together on improving inventions. Do you think that today's inventors work in the same way, or are they more competitive with each other and more possessive of their intellectual property? Explain your answer with concrete examples.

- Some of the inventors were regarded as "crazy" by the general public. (Ex: Fulton) What type of person does it take to pursue an idea that others do not think is possible? After reading about several inventors from any time or place in history, create a list of some of the key qualities or personality traits which many inventors seem to have in common.

- Many of the inventions presented in this book filled an important need in saving time, labor, and expense over the previous method of doing that task. Make a chart or graph of the man-hours and/or costs saved by several inventions such as the cotton gin, the elevator, the data processing machine, or others.

- Comment on this statement about the automobile made in 1899.

    "The ordinary 'horseless carriage' will never, of
    course, come into as common use as the bicycle."
    — *Literary Digest,* 1899

- Some think that progress in transportation was the major achievement of the 19th century. Others argue for the improved technology in the field of communications. What do you think was more important? Why?

- How frustrating must it be to know that something can be done to improve an invention, but not being able to find the exact method to implement the idea? Explain your answer with an example from your own experience, if possible.

- What key benefits did the development of the assembly line have in the growth of industry? Were there any drawbacks?

The Inventions and Discoveries of Benjamin Franklin
By Robert Ripley, From "Ripley's New Believe it or Not!" 1931

He was the first American philosopher.
He was the first American ambassador.
He invented the harmonica.
He invented the rocking chair.
He invented the street lamp.
He was the first political cartoonist.
He was the best swimmer of his time.
He originated the first circulating library.
He discovered the Gulf Stream.
He invented the lightning conductor.
He is the originator of Daylight Saving Time.
He was four times president of Pennsylvania.
He introduced newspaper carrying by mail.
He first charted the course of northeast storms.
He originated the first street-cleaning department.
He discovered the identity of lightning and electricity.
He was the first American wise-cracker and epigrammatist.
He invented commercial advertising.
He was the inventor of double spectacles.
He was the author of the Abbreviated English Prayer Book.
He was the first reformer of English spelling.
He was the first to discover that exhaled air is poisonous.
He gave the first explanation of the Aurora Borealis.
He is the father of modern dentistry.
He organized the first fire department.
He was the founder of the Democratic party.
He established the modern post-office system.
He invented the Franklin stove.
He invented the white duck clothing used in tropical climates.
He was the first to use illustrations in advertising.
He was a pioneer of the modern voting system for Congress.
He introduced the yellow willow and broom corn into America.
He was the first man to understand the nature of a cold.
He originated the first system of ventilation.
He was the inventor of Plaster of Paris for fertilizing.

- Choose one of the items above to research and report on to the class.

Sample Document

> **THE NORTHWEST MAGAZINE, FEBRUARY, 1892.**
> **Inventions of the Future.**
>
> In a recent newspaper interview Mr. Thomas A. Edison, in response to the query whether the inventions of the next fifty years will equal those of the past fifty years, replied: "I see no reason why they should not, It seems to me that we are at the beginning of inventions. We are discovering new principles, new powers, and new materials every day, and no one can predict the possibilities of the future. Take electricity. When we get electricity from coal, a lump as big as this tumbler will light and heat a whole house for hours, and a basketful would run a factory a whole day. In the generation of steam, we only get fourteen per cent of the energy of the coal. In electricity we get ninety-six per cent. When we get electrical power direct from coal a few hundred pounds will carry you across the Atlantic and a few basketfuls will take a railroad train from New York to San Francisco. I believe this to be one of the great problems of the future, and I have no doubt but that it will be solved. I have been working on it for years, but I haven't got it yet. When it does come it will revolutionize everything. It will cheapen everything, and it will be the greatest invention of modern times. As it is now we have to burn the coal to get the steam, and the steam gives us the power which runs the dynamo and produces the electricity. We have by no means reached the perfection of the telephone." Mr. Edison went on. "Improvements are being made all the time, and the day will come when every one will have his telephone. Long distance telephoning is growing, and the only restrictions of the possibilities of the telephone is in the sympathetic contact of the electrical wire with the rest of nature. If the single wire could be placed so high above the earth that it would not touch the mountain tops you could whisper around the world and you could sing a song in London and have it heard in Pekin. Wherever we get the wire comparatively free from contact with the earth, distance seems to make no difference, and on a Government line 1,000 miles long over a treeless country in Arizona we got a better telephone connection than we get now between New York and Philadelphia. If we could have a telephone from the earth to the sun—I mean a wire—we could send sounds there with perfect ease; and with the phonograph, were our language universal, we could make a speech here and have it recorded and reproduced in any of the great planetary bodies."

- Edison had a lot to say that was right on target. Find his comments in this article which became a reality in the years after his interview.
- What were some of the "new principles, new powers, and new materials" to which Edison was referring in the article?
- Use the worksheet on page 53 to evaluate this document.

Written Document Worksheet

Based on Worksheet from *Teaching with Documents*,
National Archives and Records Administration

1. **Type of document:**
   - ❏ Newspaper
   - ❏ Letter
   - ❏ Congressional Record
   - ❏ Memo
   - ❏ Journal
   - ❏ Diary
   - ❏ Telegram
   - ❏ Ship Manifest
   - ❏ Press Release
   - ❏ Report
   - ❏ Advertisement
   - ❏ Patent
   - ❏ Deed
   - ❏ Census Report
   - ❏ Interview

2. **Unique Characteristics of the Document:**
   - ❏ Interesting Stationery
   - ❏ Unusual Fold Marks
   - ❏ "CLASSIFIED" Stamp
   - ❏ Typed
   - ❏ "Copy"
   - ❏ "RECEIVED" Stamp
   - ❏ Handwritten
   - ❏ Written Notations
   - ❏ "TOP SECRET" Stamp
   - ❏ Official

3. **Date(s) of Document:**   ❏ No Date

4. **Author of Document:**   **Position:**

5. **For what audience was the document written?**

6. **In your opinion, what are the 3 most important points of the document?**
   a.
   b.
   c.

7. **Why do you think the document was written?**

8. **Choose a quote from the document that helped you to know why it was written:**

9. **Write down two clues which you got from the document that tell you something about life in the U.S. at the time it was written:**

10. **Write a question to the author that you feel is unanswered:**

11. **What do you think the response to the document was?**

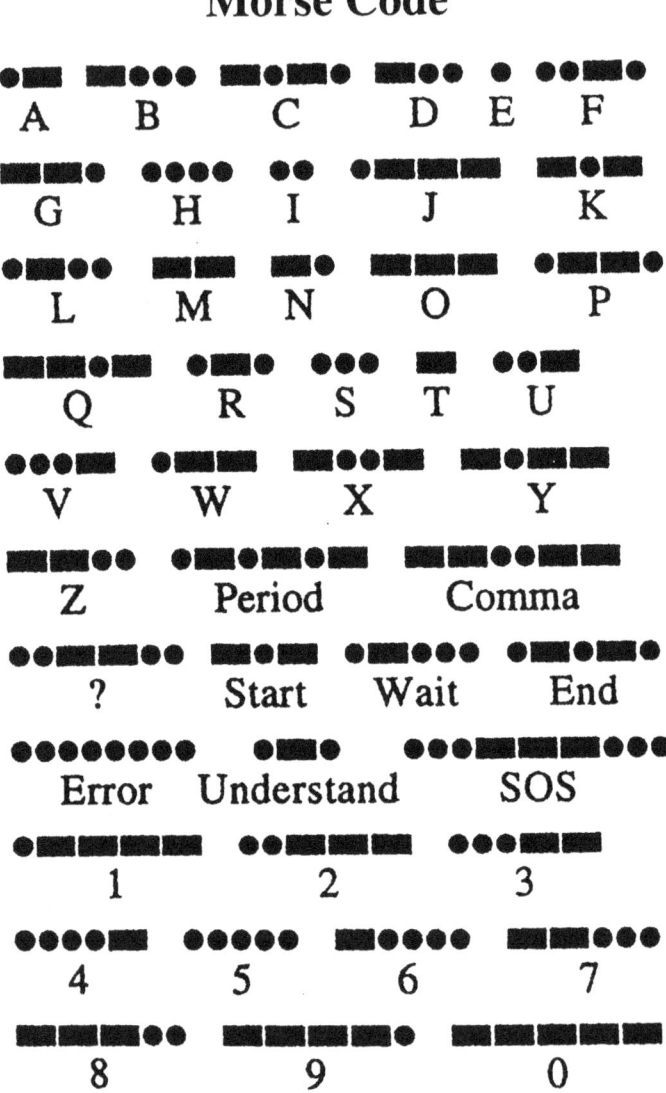

The alphabet, numbers, and commands of the Morse Code, used to transmit telegraph messages by a series of dots and dashes

- Write a letter in Morse Code to the class and see who can decode it. Better yet, try it with a real telegraph key.

- How are the letters and words in a message separated from each other?

Sample Cartoon

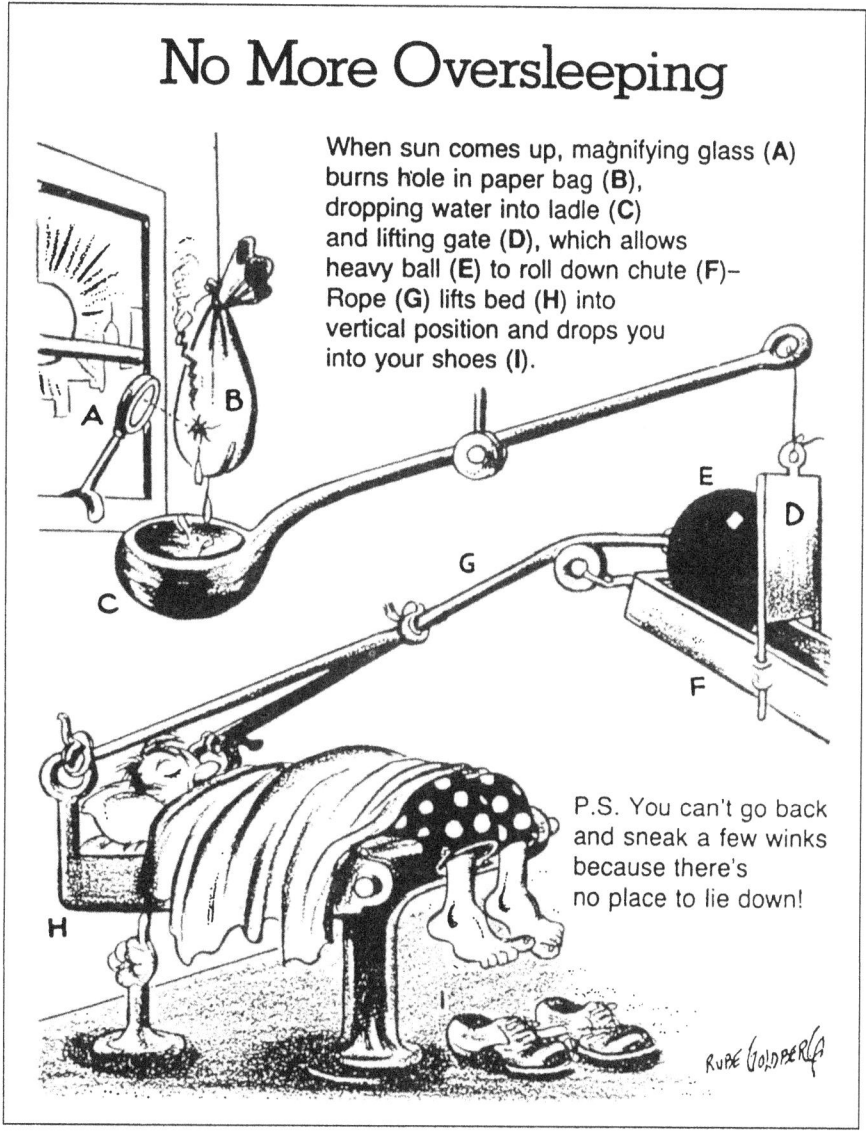

Source: Charles Keller, *The Best of Rube Goldberg*. Englewood Cliffs: Prentice-Hall, 1944, p. 116.

Rube Goldberg inventions have amused people for generations. Their intricate configuration of items **complicates the simple**. A Rube Goldberg invention reverses the normal pattern of problem-solving by seeking to make answers difficult to obtain. However, everything is done with a tongue-in-cheek approach. Above is an example of a typical Rube Goldberg discovery.

- After examining this cartoon, use the same method of cause and effect to illustrate your own device for doing some task.

Suggested Further Reading

Coleman, Wim, and Perrin, Pat. *Aviation: Early Flight in America,* Carlisle, MA: Discovery Enterprises, Ltd., 1999.

Haskins, James. *Outward Dreams: Black Inventors and their Inventions*, New York: Walker & Company, 1991.

James, Portia P. *The Real McCoy: African-American Invention and Innovation*, Washington, D.C.: Smithsonian Institution Press, 1989.

King, David C. *Thomas Alva Edison: The King of Inventors,* Carlisle, MA: Discovery Enterprises, Ltd., 1997.

King, David C. *The Age of Technology: 19th Century American Inventors*, Carlisle, MA: Discovery Enterprises, Ltd., 1997.

Lafferty, Peter. *The Inventor Through History*, New York: Thompson Learning, 1993.

Norman, Bruce. *The Inventing of America*, New York: Taplinger Publishing Company, 1976.

Richardson, Robert O. *The Weird and Wondrous World of Invention*, New York: Sterling Publishing Co., 1990.

Showell, Ellen H. and Amram, Fred M. B. *From Indian Corn to Outer Space: Women Invent America,* Peterborough, NH: Cobblestone Publishing, Inc., 1995.

Stanley, Autumn. *Mothers and Daughters of Invention: Notes for a Revised History of Technology*, Metuchen, NJ: Scarecrow Press, 1993.

Suggested Web Sites

The Inventors Museum — www.inventorsmuseum.com

Eli Whitney Museum — www.eliwhitney.org/main.htm

Benjamin Franklin — library.advanced.org/22254/home.htm

American history/inventors — americanhistory.about.com/index.htm

Amer. Computer Museum — www.compustory.com

Scientific & Medical... — www.americanartifacts.com/smma/index.htm

National Archives — www.nara.gov/education/

Library of Congress — lcweb2.loc.gov/ammem/ammemhome.html

Making of America — www.hti.umich.edu

www.ingramcontent.com/pod-product-compliance
Lightning Source LLC
Chambersburg PA
CBHW081022040426
42444CB00014B/3314